I seem to have gotten ahead of myself.

I seem to have talked myself

3

All rights reserved

No part of this book may be reproduced in any form or by any electronic or mechanical means, including information storage and retrieval systems, without written permission from the author, except for the use of brief quotations in a book review.

ISBN: 978-1-7380632-0-8

Written + illustrated

By: John Ross

Special Thanks

To:

Taylor Ironmonger

Stephen Vincelli

Burke Brockelbank

Denise + Allan Ross

Idioms are phrases that are not meant to be taken **literally** but instead, have widely understood figurative meanings.

Inside this book is a collection of over

100

playful, hand drawn illustrations of some of English's most popular idioms. Try to guess the idiom represented by the drawing on each page, if you get stuck, all the answers are at the back!

Good luck.

Whoa, not so fast!

Why is it always in my side?

You don't know the half of it.

Can we keep em'?

What is your conclusion?

Could I just have a moment of your time.

15

This should get your attention.

16

This is the most beautiful bush I've ever seen.

How Spontaneous!!

Just a few more boxes to go...

Make sure to go right to the edge.

Now it's all out there...

21

That's 27 feet   or

8.2 meters

| | | | 9 | 10

BAR—

nevermind.

Take a deeeeep breath, and pull.

I can only hold them for so long.

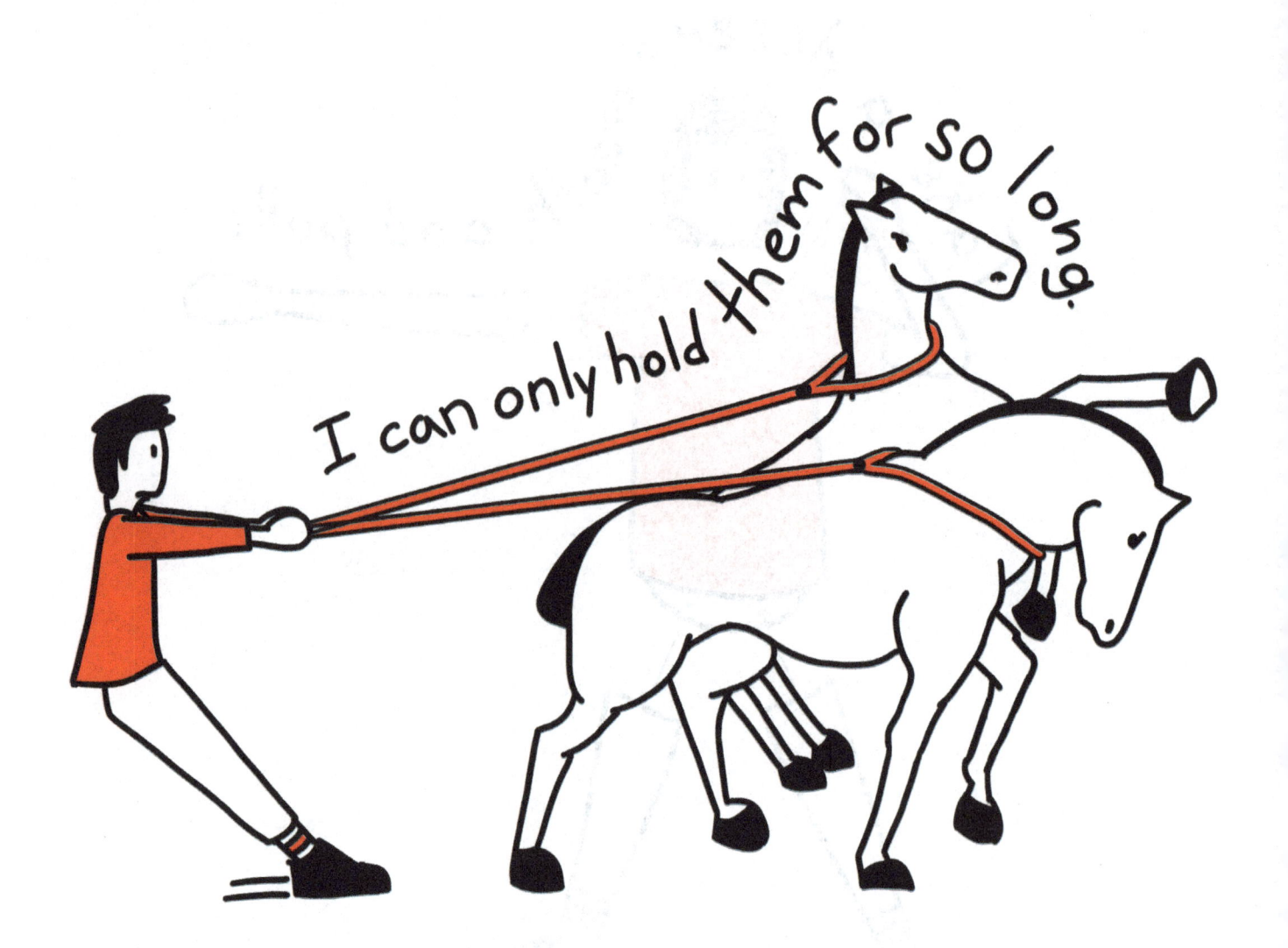

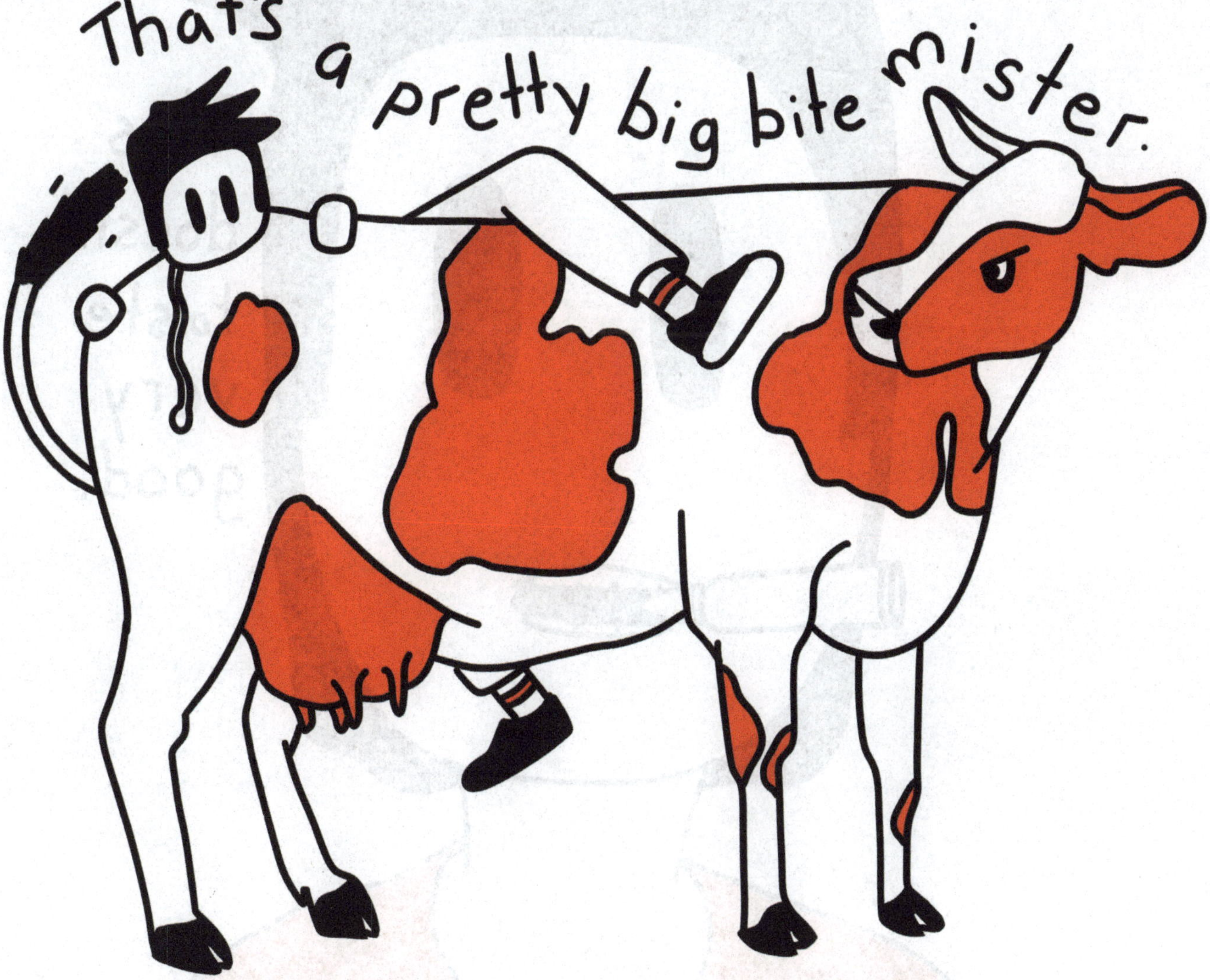
That's a pretty big bite mister.

This doesn't taste very good.

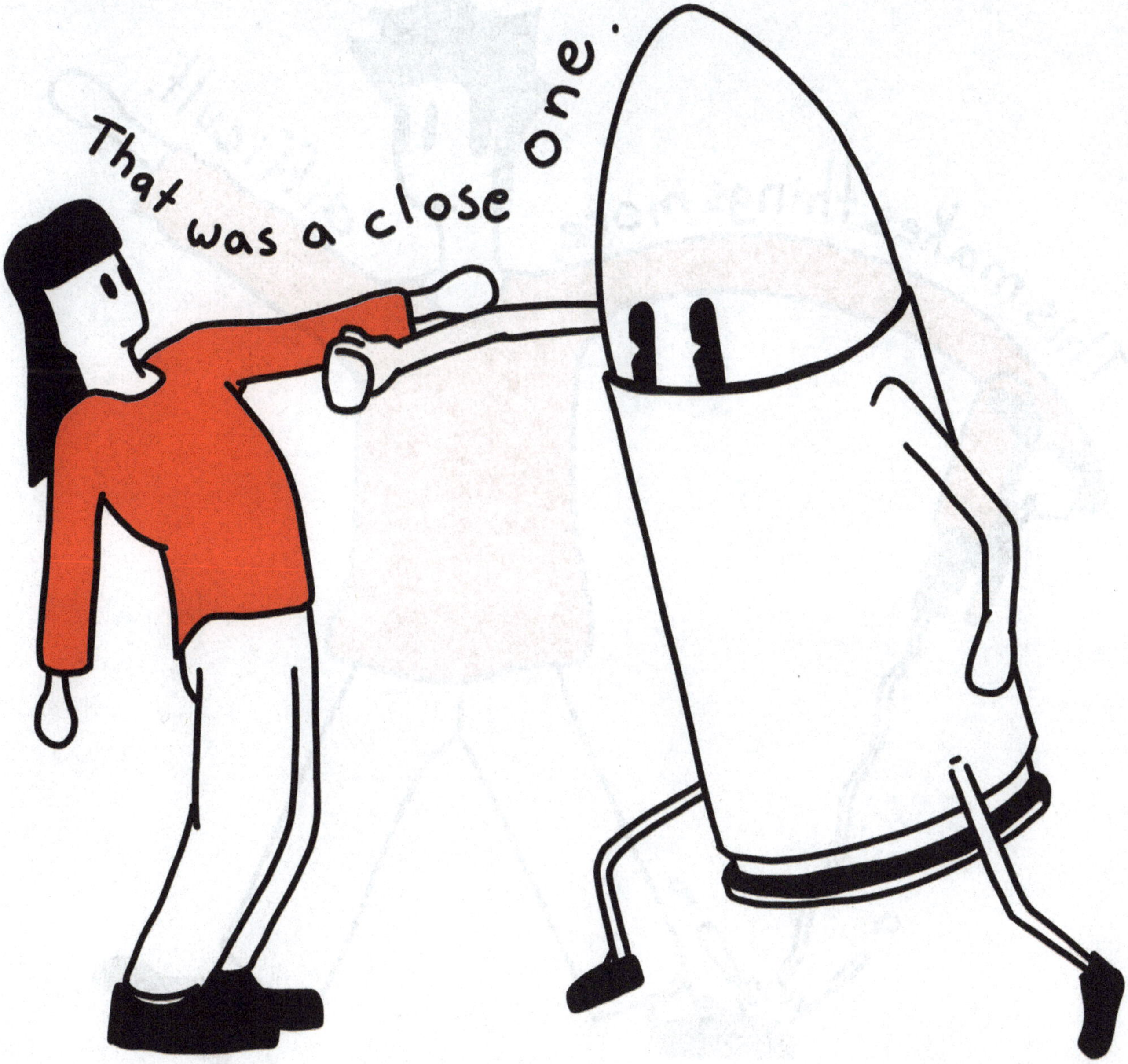
That was a close one.

This makes things more, difficult.

Best to get it over with.

I have to get out of here.

...on't succeed... If at first you do

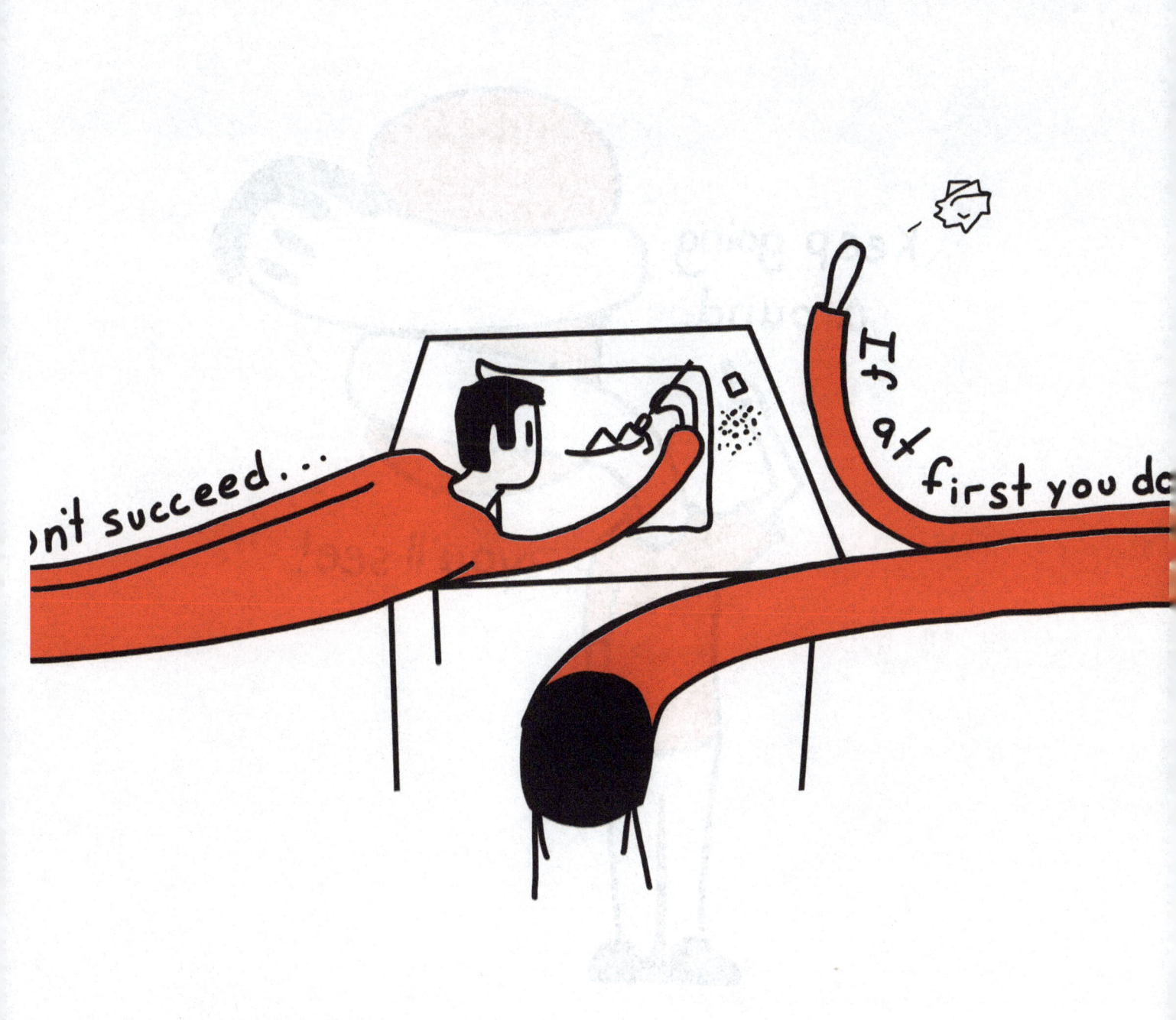

Keep going around, you'll see!

and just a pinch of lightning.

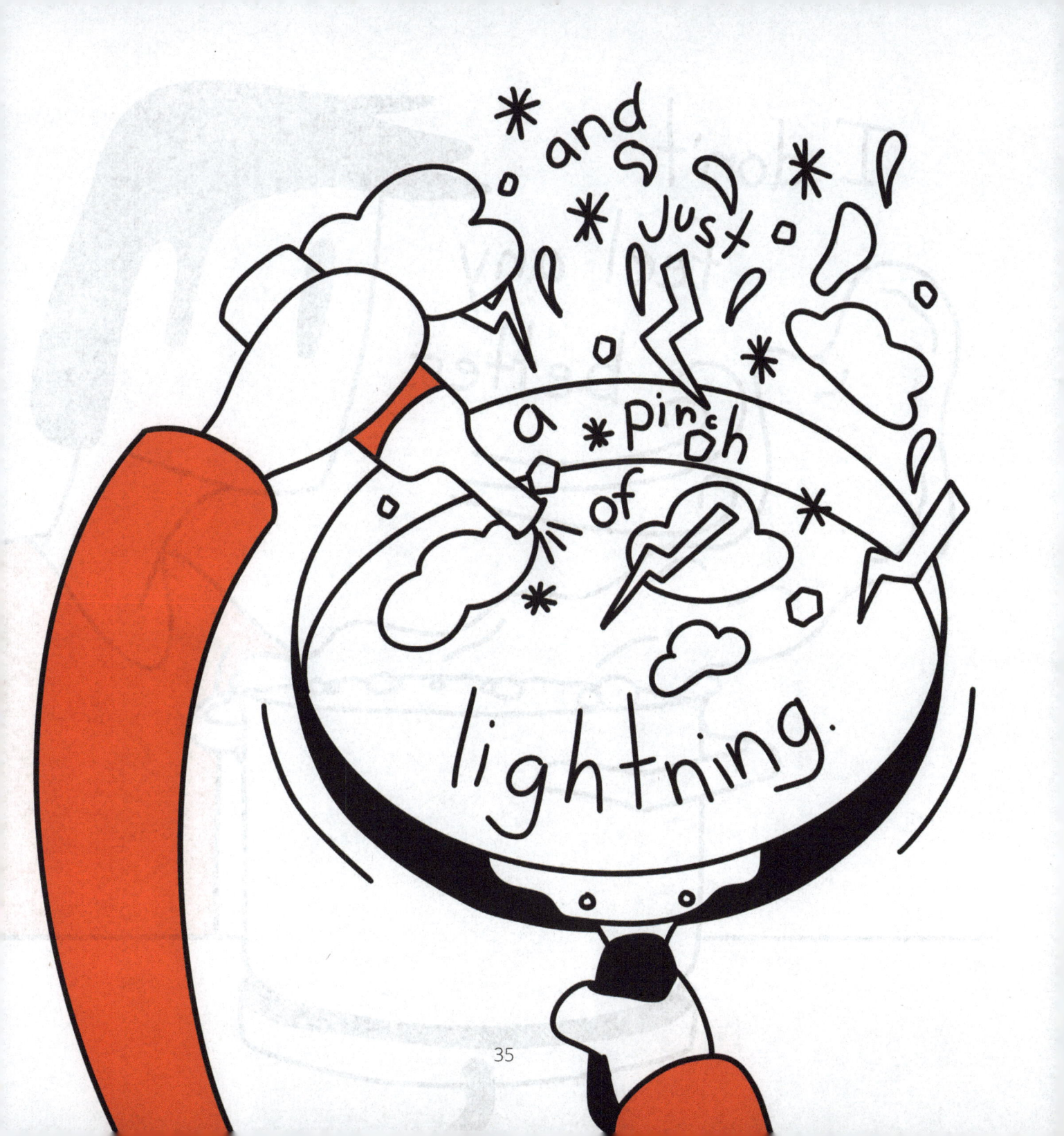

I don't feel any better.

Just give it a try!

I was just talking about you.

38

Always check the fine print.

Calm down.

Power is knowledge.

I GOT IT!

GO LONG!

This ride will be closing in five minutes.

Are you even listening to me?

Should have got a flu shot.

Must be a stuffy nose.

Never saw it coming.

Deal!

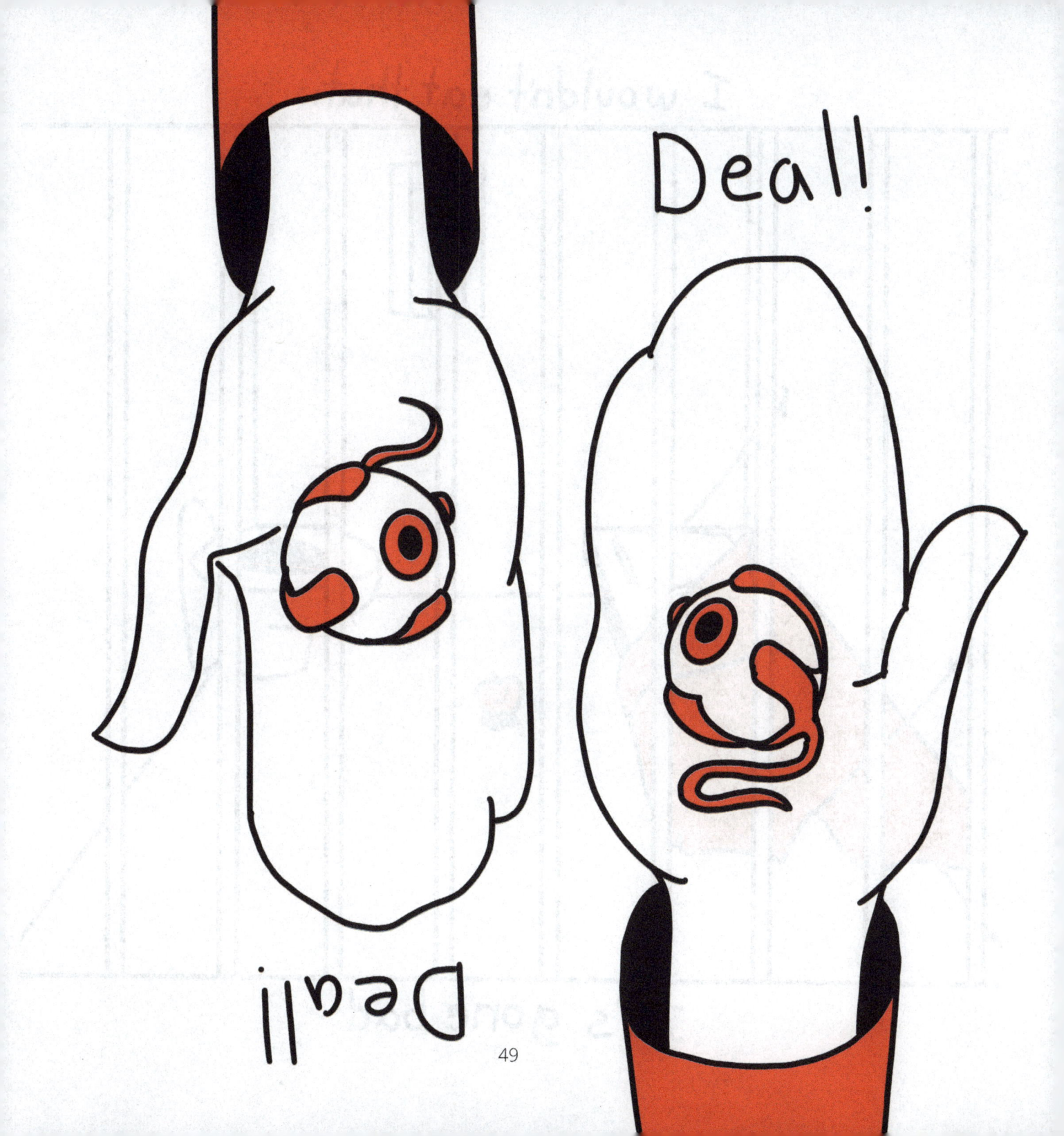

Deal!

I wouldn't eat that...

It's gone bad.

You have your mother's stem.

Everything looks the same.

No two are alike!

Can you pass the chips please?

Far away and A-OKAY.

So good

No sheet music required.

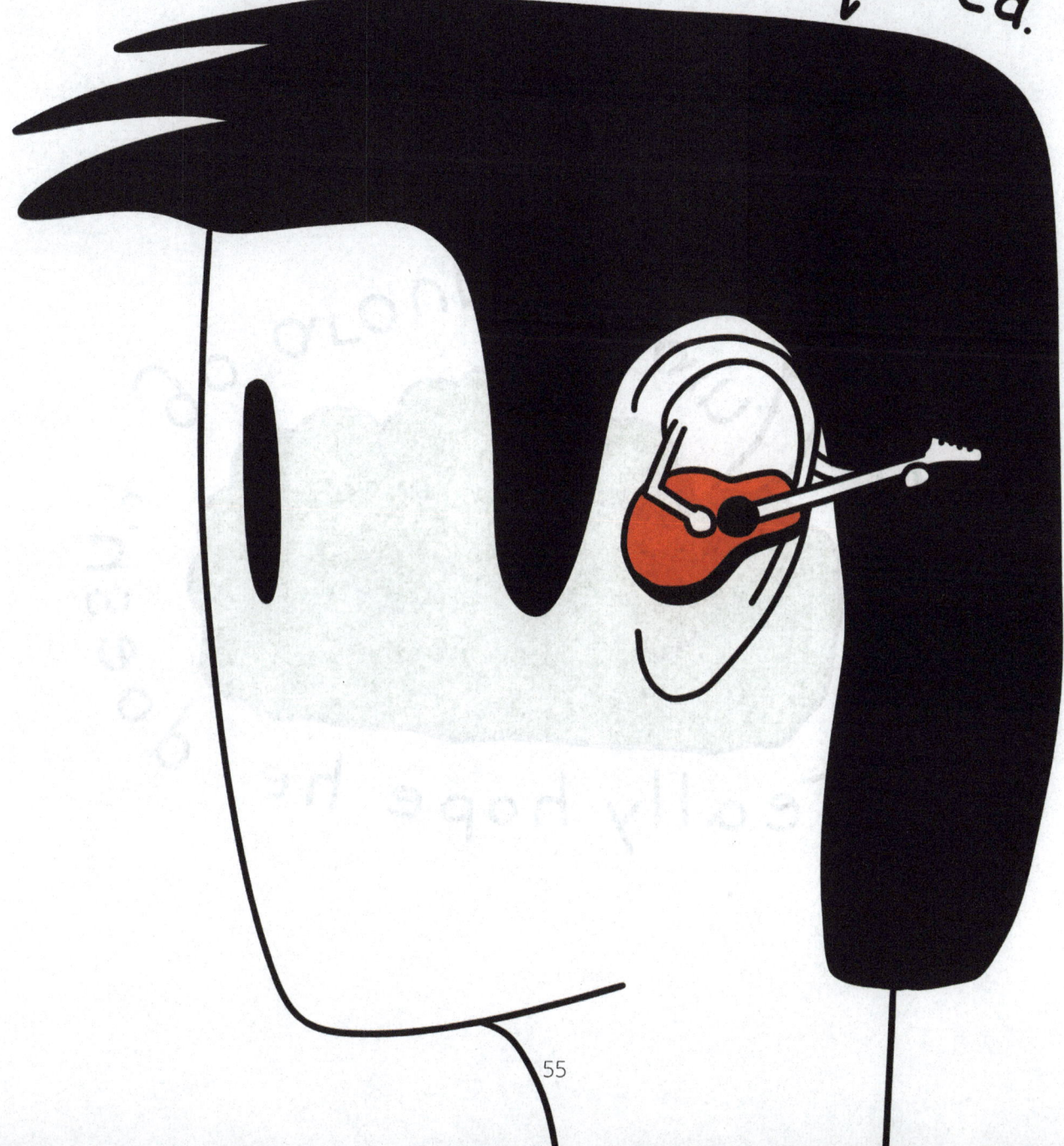

I really hope he doesn't go around again.

Even clean cuts produce poor results.

It's like they just don't want to move!

Dangerously close.

Let's not think about that.

One side is bound

to give way.

I don't want my side.

I want YOUR side.

Not the Beans!

I make the rules around here.

I would NOT like to add a gratuity.

Who can afford this?!

3 EASY PAYMENTS of 1 and 1

That money is mine.

I'd much rather the ball be on your side.

What do you think about this.

Not even worth the penny.

Did you check under the couch?

Right through the eye.

oops.

Just focus on a spot in the distance.

"Can't you see I'm working here."

I'd rather not choose.

How many more rounds?

"I've got a big one on the line!"

Be free little guy.

Can I quote you on that?

Hey! = Don't write that down!

This should keep me out of trouble.

It doesn't take much sometimes.

We are proud of you turkey.

(Don't let this stop you.

You may not like this brew.

I wouldn't go in there.

You have to admire his...

Persistence?

Resistance?

Twice as bright

for half as long.

Don't let that blow away!

Unsurprisingly,

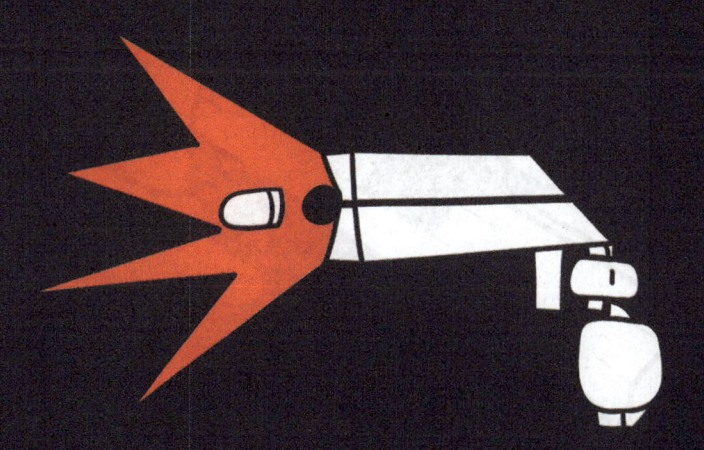

nothing was hit.

Those will kill you ya know.

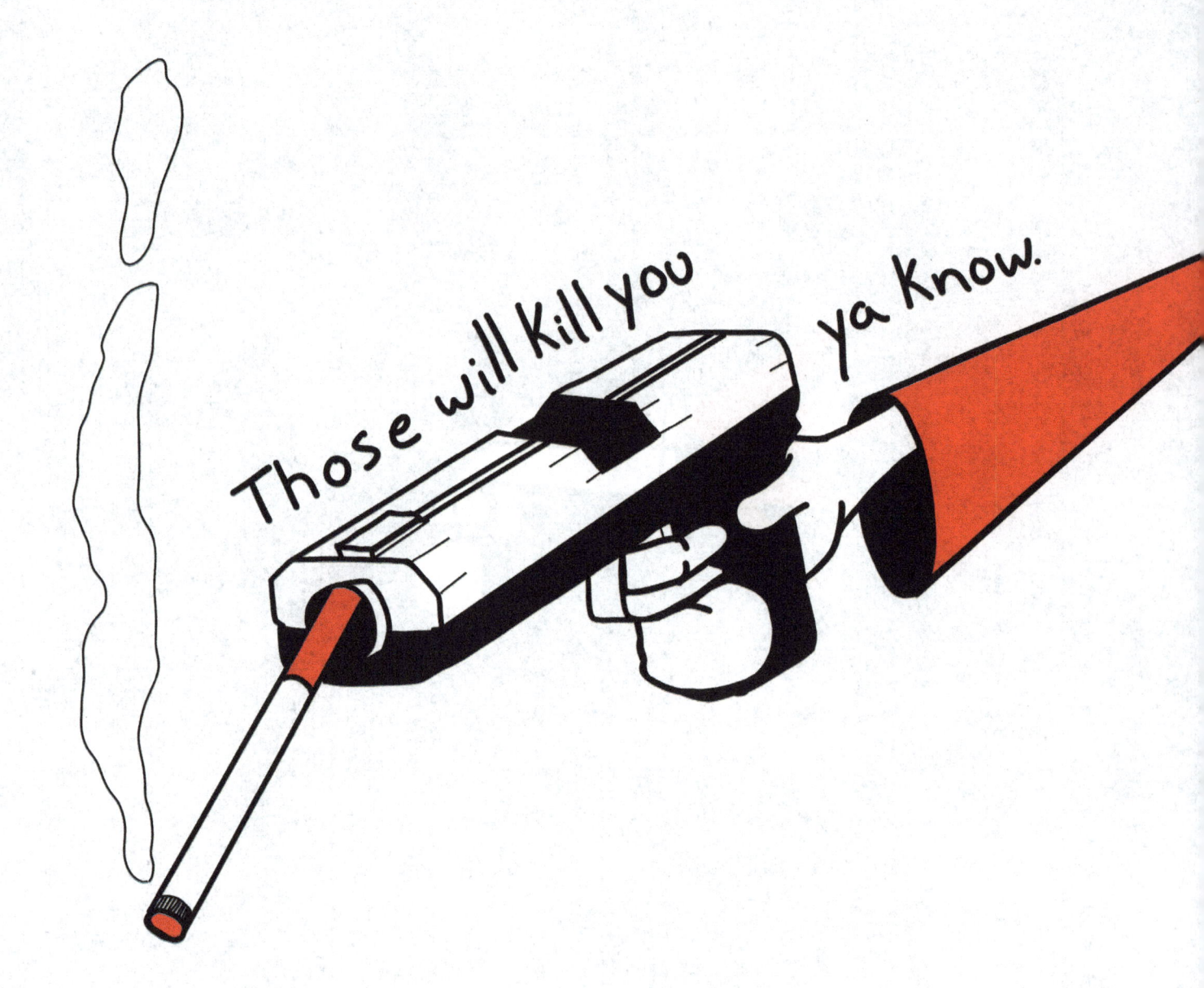

This fish is a clue.

This little guy was NOT EASY to find.

Now you must flop to survive.

There's room for one more beside me!

Let me chew on this.

97

Pancakes

Do they have any syrup at least?

You're smart, you can get out of this.

Go get your own!

Which one was yours again?

Sometimes you must go around.

It's easier if you gain their trust.

Can you take it higher?

Better than the bar.

Looks like we need a new JAR.

Don't look down...

Down to my last one.

Helps me fall asleep.

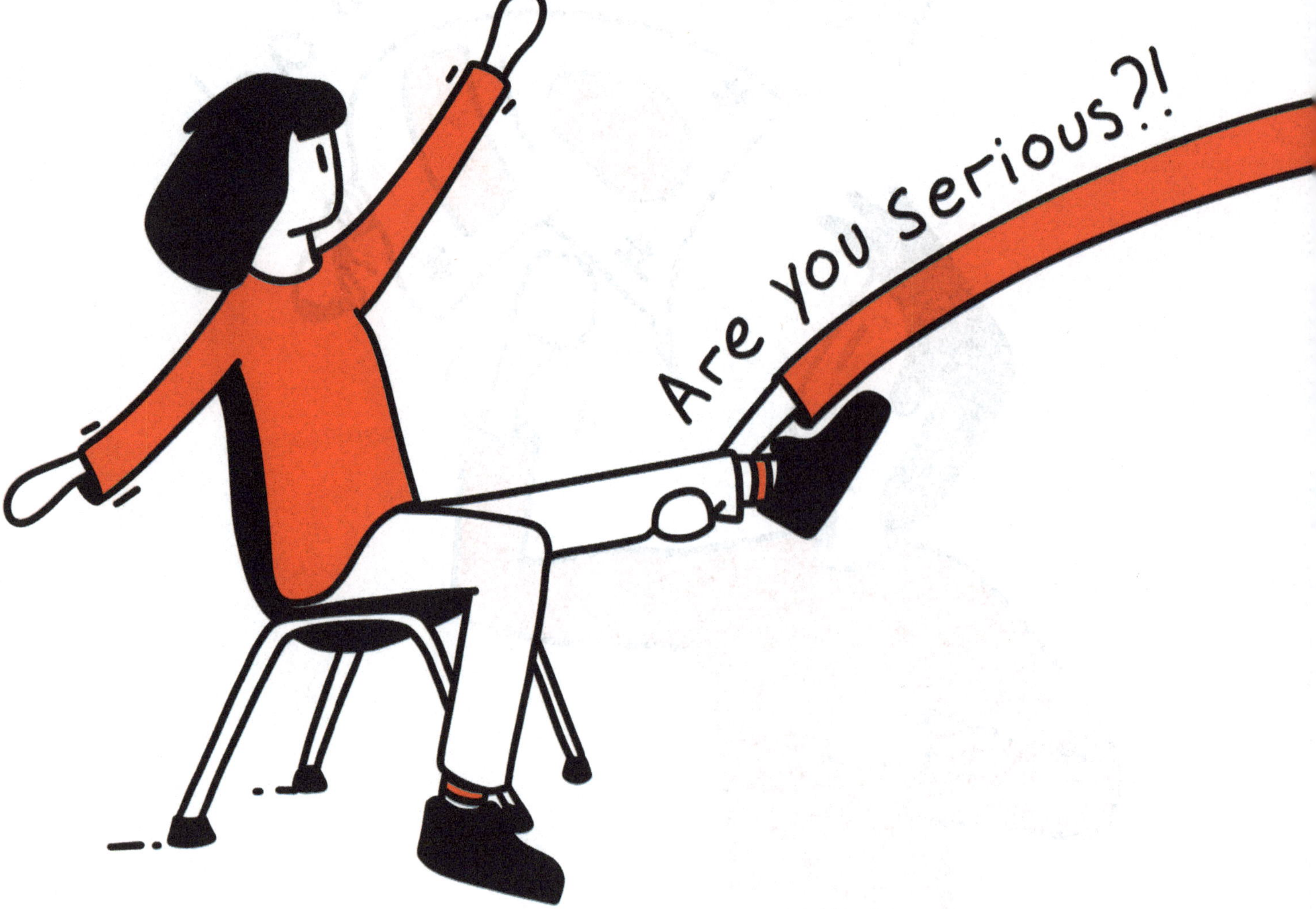
Are you Serious?!

Amazing and horrible at the same time.

I'll just get to the point.

I don't like this music.

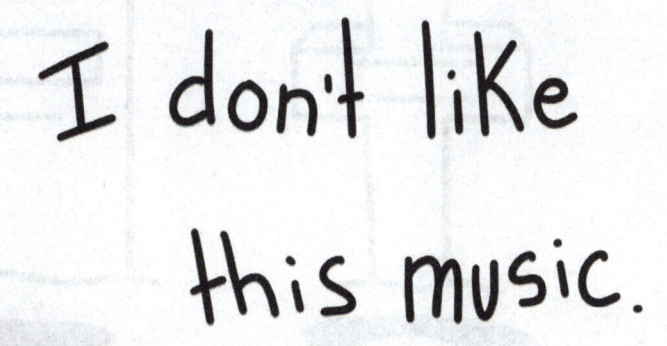

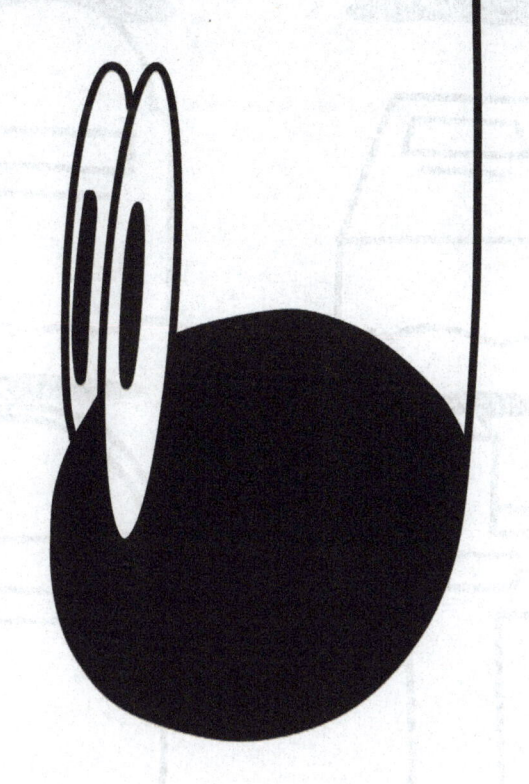

Last one!

You're almost there.

It's not a race to the end.

Did I miss the turn?

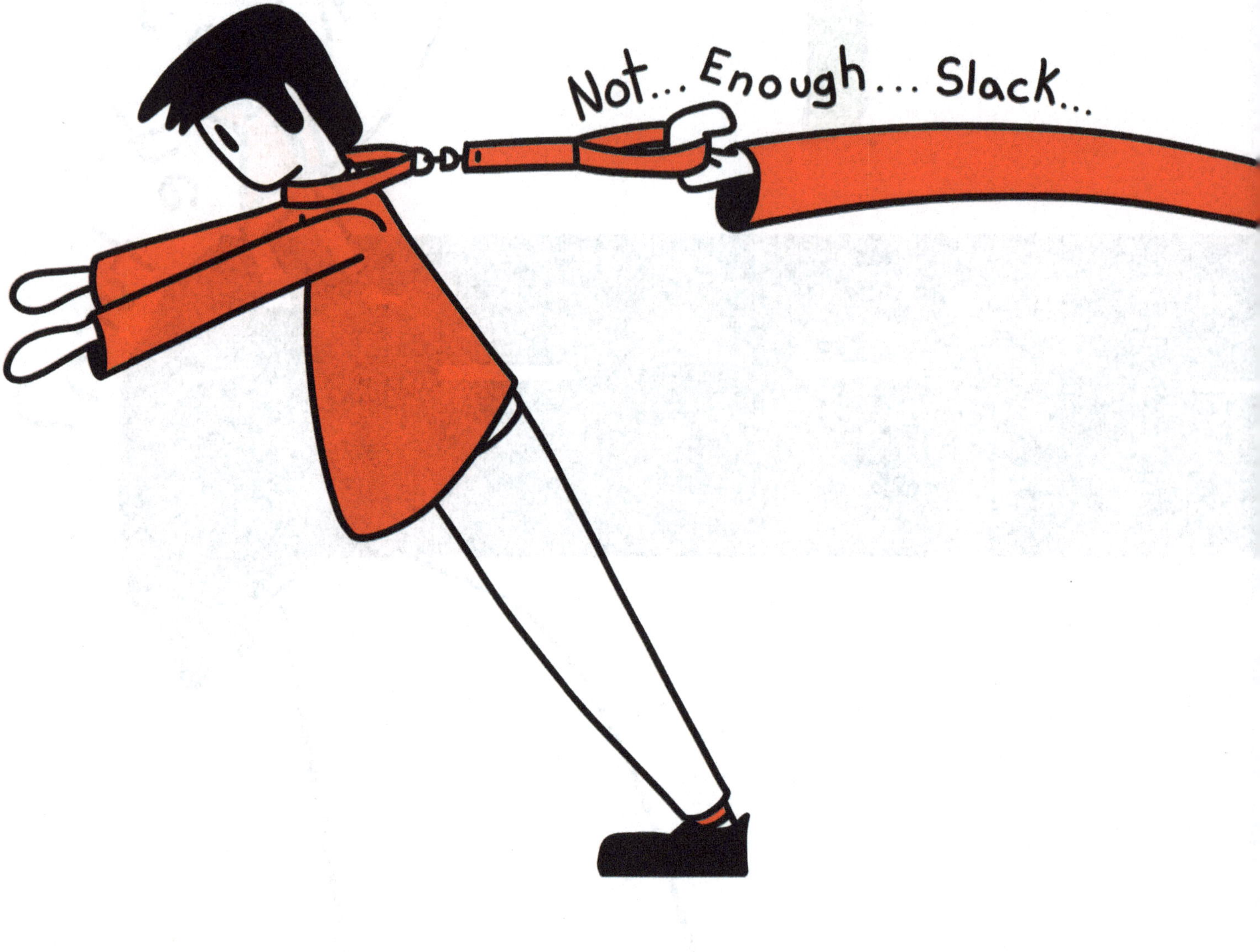
Not... Enough... Slack...

Honey... I'm home!

I'm never going back in there.

I sincerely thank you for reading.

The Answers

Put the cart before the horse 1
To reverse the proper order or procedure of something
Copyright page 4
Author page 5
Special thanks 6
What is an idiom? 7
Preface 8
Break a leg 9
Good luck!
Jump the gun 10
To act before the proper time
Thorn in one's side 11
A continuous problem or annoyance

Tip of the iceberg 12
Something is only a small part of a much bigger situation

Raining cats and dogs 13
When it's raining very hard

Test the water/s 14
To find out the reaction to an action/idea before committing to it

Foot in the door 15
To make a small but successful start at something

Break the ice 16
To say or do something that gets you past the initial awkwardness of meeting someone new

Rose coloured glasses 17
An unrealisticly positive attitude that fails to notice the negatives of a situation

At the drop of a hat 18
To do something immediately and without delay

Bend over backwards 19
To work extra hard to make something happen, or help someone to make them happy

Butter someone up 20
To flatter or praise someone as a means of gaining their help or support

Pour one's heart out 21
To speak openly with someone about your deeply felt emotions

The whole nine yards. 22
To want, have, or do everything in a particular situation

Barking up the wrong tree 24
To pursue a mistaken or misguided line of thought or course of action

Pull yourself together 25
To regain control of an emotional state

Hold your horses 26
To wait or slow down

Bite off more than you can chew 27
To be unable to fulfill an obligation

Bite the bullet 28
To do something unpleasant or difficult because it is necessary even though you would like to avoid it

Dodge a bullet 29
To narrowly avoid an undesirable event

Shoot oneself in the foot 30
To inadvertently make a situation worse for oneself

A tough pill to swallow 31
To experience something that is hard or difficult to accept

Back against the wall 32
To be in a tough situation in which one is forced to act

Back to the drawing board 33
To start a new plan, idea, or proposal that was previously unsuccessful

Wrap your head around it 34
To accept or understand something strange or challenging

Cooking up a storm 35
Cooking a large quantity of food with skill and passion

Blow off steam 36
An act meant to decrease pent-up energy or strong emotions

Twist someone's arm 37
To persuade someone to do something that they are or might be reluctant to do

Speak of the devil 38
When someone appears moments after being mentioned

The devil is in the details 39
The details of a matter can have a big, often negative, impact

Bent out of shape 40
To be angry or annoyed

Hit the books 41
To read or study

Catch the time 42
To know what time it is

Pass the time 43
To do something in order to make a waiting period more enjoyable

Time flies when you're having fun 44
Time appears to pass more quickly when engaged in something one enjoys

Head in the clouds 45
To be disconnected from reality or daydreaming
Under the weather 46
To feel slightly unwell
Under someone's nose 47
To commit an act openly and in front of someone without them noticing
Stab someone in the back 48
To betray someone's trust through a harmful act
An eye for an eye 49
The idea that the punishment should fit the crime
A bad apple 50
A bad or corrupt person in a group, often tarnishing the rest of the group's reputation
The apple doesn't fall far from the tree. 51
A child grows up to be similar to its parents
Comparing apples to oranges 52
An invalid comparison of two items due to their difference
Couch potato 53
Someone who doesn't have an active life and spends a lot of time watching TV
So far so good 54
Everything has been going well up until this point
Play it by ear 55
To proceed instinctively and spontaneously according to the situation
Beat around the bush 56
To avoid talking about the point of a matter
Cut corners 57
To do something in the easiest, quickest, or cheapest way, often omitting something important
Drag one's feet 58
To be deliberately slow to act
Toe the line 59
To follow rules and orders, without causing trouble
We'll cross that bridge when we come to it 60
To deal with a situation only once it occurs

Between a rock and a hard place 61
To be in a tough situation faced with two equally difficult alternatives

The grass is always greener on the other side of the fence 62
The things or situations one doesn't have are more appealing than their own

Spill the beans. 63
To inadvertently or indiscreetly disclose private or confidential information

Rule of thumb 64
A guide or procedure based on experience and common sense

Pay through the nose 65
To pay much more than a fair price for something

Costs an arm and a leg 66
Used to say something is very expensive

A run for one's money 67
To make it difficult for one to win due to strong competition

The ball is in your court 68
It is up to you to make the next decision

Bounce something off someone 69
To tell someone something to find out what they think

A penny for your thoughts 70
To ask someone what they are thinking, especially when they are quiet or pensive

Leave no stone unturned 71
To do everything possible to find or solve something

Thread the needle 72
To apply a lot of care and concentration in a difficult or tight position

Dropped the ball. 73
To make an error or miss an opportunity

On the ball 74
To be alert, focused, and able to react to something at any moment

On the clock. 75
To be working, or getting paid

On the fence 76
To be unable to make a decision between two things

On the ropes 77
To be helpless and on the verge of defeat
On the hook 78
To be caught in a bad situation or owe someone money
Off the hook 79
To no longer be responsible for or involved in an obligation
On the record 80
To be willing to state something publicly
Off the record 81
To state something privately, not to be shared
On the wagon 82
To be abstaining from bad habits
Off the wagon 83
To go back to abusing bad habits after a period of abstinence
Cold turkey 84
To withdraw suddenly from an addiction
Hang in there 85
To push through something difficult
Storm is brewing 86
To predict the coming of a storm or emotional reaction
Out of hand 87
When a situation is out of control
Stick to one's guns 88
To refuse to change actions or beliefs despite criticism
Burn the candle from both ends 89
To overextend oneself and do more than one should
Throw caution to the wind 90
To do something without worrying about the risk or negative results
Shot in the dark 91
To guess something without any clues or prior knowledge
Smoking gun 92
Something that serves as indisputable evidence, especially of a crime

Red herring 93
A false clue or piece of information intended to misdirect

A needle in a haystack. 94
To express when something is impossible or difficult to find

Fish out of water 95
To be in an uncomfortable and unfamiliar situation

Packed like sardines 96
To be in a situation where one is in close proximity to many others

Food for thought. 97
Information, ideas, or perspectives that should be carefully considered

Selling like hotcakes 98
When something is selling quickly and in large quantities

Smart cookie 99
An intelligent person who makes good decisions

Not one's cup of tea 100
To not like or be interested in something

The glass is half full/half empty 101
To focus solely on the negatives or positives of a situation, while ignoring the opposite

Workaround 102
To find a way to overcome a problem without completely solving it

Kill two birds with one stone 103
To achieve two things in a single action

Raise the bar 104
To increase the standard

Bar none. 105
To state something is true without exception

Spread oneself thin 106
To try to do too many things at the same time to the detriment of them all

Hanging by a thread 107
To be in a dangerous situation, in which a slight change could have catastrophic results

The last straw 108
A series of undesirable events causing one to realize they can no longer accept a given situation

Hit the sack **109**
To go to bed/sleep

Pull one's leg **110**
To tease someone, often by persuading them to believe something that isn't true

When pigs fly **111**
To express to someone that something will probably never happen

To make a long story short **112**
To provide the most important points rather than going into a long explanation

Face the music **113**
To accept the unpleasant consequences of one's actions

Cats have nine lives **114**
Cats are lucky and always seem to survive fatal situations

Light at the end of the tunnel **115**
To see a resolution to a long and difficult situation

End of one's rope **116**
To be at the limit of one's patience

End of the road **117**
The point at which one can no longer continue

On a short leash **118**
Keeping someone or something under close control and supervision

Bring home the bacon **119**
To earn money to provide the necessities of life

Out of the woods **120**
To be out of the prior difficulties and challenges

Thank you for reading **121**
Answers **122**
Missed the boat **132**
To have missed an opportunity due to slow action

131

we've got a schedule to keep!

Made in United States
North Haven, CT
19 December 2024